FLY-FISH
THE SURF

Lee R. Baermann

All inquiries should be addressed to:
Frank Amato Publications, Inc.
P.O. Box 82112
Portland, Oregon 97282
(503) 653-8108
www.AmatoBooks.com

ISBN-13: 978-1-57188-519-7
UPC: 0-81127-00370-9
Printed in Singapore

10 9 8 7 6 5 4 3 2 1

FLY-FISH
THE SURF

Lee R. Baermann

FAP

**Frank Amato
Publications**

Table of Contents

Acknowledgments

It could have happened so much differently but all the credit has to go to my mother for moving to Southern California in 1960. Even better was that she didn't move to the desert but settled on the laid-back beach lifestyle. Thanks, Lu.

And anyone who is married knows that you don't spend copious amounts of time on the wet sand without having a loving and understanding wife. Karen may call my passion for fly-fishing on the beach an obsession but even she can now read water . . . osmosis? She also ignores the reels, rods and flies that litter our house, but it is not my fault.

I blame Tim Rajeff and the crew at Rajeff Sports for supplying me with the rods and lines I need to be on the water just about every day, be it at home in the surf or the warm waters of the Sea of Cortez.

Ryan Harrison at Waterworks-Lamson gets some of the blame as well because he has sent me the reels I need to fish for carp, largemouth bass, roosterfish, sailfish and mako sharks as well as the species of the surf. Those reels also see service with my clients on the wet sand so they have to hold up to a grueling schedule of use.

My feet stay happy because a guy like David Zasloff of Sockwa listens and makes the most comfortable and sand-free surf shoe.

Gary Fisher and Nelz of Solarez have the best UV epoxy going out there so that leaves me more time to fish and their UV light rocks.

And finally there's Eric Huff. He understands the simplification of fishing, be it million-dollar marlin tournaments or playing on the wet sand. He's a friend, a sounding board and a wealth of fishing knowledge, thanks buddy.

Introduction

"Happiness does not come from doing easy work but from the afterglow of satisfaction that comes after the achievement of a difficult task that demanded our best."

—Theodore Isaac Rubin

My whole life I've always gravitated to doing things the hard way. I don't know if this is a character flaw or an honorable quest to make me a better person…or am I an idiot? Either way you slice it, casting a fly rod ain't easy.

As a child I grew up at Hollywood Beach in Oxnard California so sand has been in my veins forever, not to mention in my food, hair and clothes. Growing up at the beach in the 60's was a "kids and dogs running wild" proposition. I can remember being in the 3rd grade and walking down the street with my friends, each one of us carrying a BB gun or bow and real arrows. We were heading to the huge sand dunes to hunt lizards. Often a Sheriff's cruiser would come by and the Officer would say, "How's it going boys?" and be off with a wave. Nowadays four eight year olds with arrows and guns would be whisked away only to be sent home with angry parents and without their 'toys'. As for the dogs? Sometimes we would not see ours for 2 or 3 days and when we did see her, she was covered in the tacky black slime of the local canals where she had been chasing ducks and squirrels.

When not playing and looking for our dog, we would go to the local liquor store and pay 50 cents for a drop line to fish the harbor. The dredging of the Channel Island Harbor started in 1960 and finished in that incarnation in 1965. There were very few docks, with most boats simply moored near the newly formed rock shorelines. The few docks that did exist at this time were our hangout during summer and other days we thought to be good fishing days. Access was not denied and no one did anything to lose that access.

We would pull mussels off the rocks and pilings, crack them open with either our palms or a swift stomp of our barefooted heel.

You had to get good at pulling back at the perfect time or you spent time pulling shell out of your foot. We caught lots of fish this way, attaching the mussel to the lone hook supplied with your drop line.

This drop line was a yellow plastic frame wrapped with a green cord with a length of fishing line secured to the end. A single egg sinker was connected to the green cord. We fished and fished and occasionally pulled shell out of our palms or feet but it was a glorious time to be a kid.

My brother Dale and I after some beach fishing. I let him hold the bigger perch... sure I did; circa 1965.

To catch a glimpse of this harbor, watch the 1963 classic "It's a Mad Mad Mad Mad World". When Spencer Tracy's character flees with the suitcase of money he attempts to back into a garage near the water but is spotted and leaves. This was filmed over two days using the Harbor Master's home on the Silverstarnd Beach side of the harbor. Near the other side of the harbor you can see how the boats were moored and not docked. Oh, and we peeked through the backyard fence and watched them shoot craps between set-up and takes.

As I got older, early teens, I looked for more challenging ways to fish so we got small trout fishing spinning rods. By now the harbor was becoming a busy place, many docks had been installed and it was getting difficult to find ones we could fish from so we ventured to the wet sand and the surf. Things moved quickly from there and we, my brother and I, got 12-foot surf rods to cast far out past the waves. We didn't stay with this for long because standing there, head pointed skyward watching the tip of a rod was boring as anything short of having to watch paint dry.

By now we were High School age and other things kept us from the wet sand, at least to fish. We surfed, swam and later partied at the same beaches we had learned to 'read water' on. This can happen as your interests change but fishing was always in the backs of our minds.

At one point I wanted to get back into surf fishing and figured the fly rod I had gotten to chase trout with would make a great device to renew my wet-sand interests. This was in the late 70's and I found an ad for sand crab flies in a fishing magazine and ordered a dozen. I fished the harbor and surrounding beaches using this set-up of a floating line and sand crab flies. I caught surf perch and even jack smelt in the harbor but didn't fare well in the surf with that floating line. By the time I had used up my flies, I once again had a change of interest.

Later, needing yet another new challenge, I went back to the fly rod for surf fishing and found new rods and reels that were more salt resistant than the trout gear I had previously used. In fact you could get a decent synthetic reel for what we had paid for that Pflueger Medalist and it was easy to find an integrated sink-tip line because they were now readily available. No more mixing and matching of whatever you had lying around—this made surf fly-fishing so much more easy to do.

That was a long time ago and the fly-fishing manufacturers have made leaps and bounds in saltwater fly gear. It is so easy to get inexpensive fly-fishing equipment that'll work so there is no excuse not to be doing it if you already fly-fish.

And therein lies the purpose of this book. I want everyone to get out on the wet sand and this book is my attempt at making your learning curve as short as possible. It also has my philosophies on this great sport. I believe that fly-fishing in the surf is the hardest way to catch these fish thus the reward is that much greater. Look, this isn't easy, not everyone can do it and many give up after not being able to conquer it the first time out. If you read the quote by Theodore Isaac Rubin and said, "Yeah, I get that" the book will make a tad more sense. Also, if by the end of this book you can find and identify one piece of structure and pull fish out of it, I've done my job.

One last thing, I have a philosophy on fly-fishing that says, "There is no right way to do this and there is no wrong way to do this, only the way you do it as long as it works for you and does not cause you pain."

1 Too Easy to Not Be Doing It

There seems to be some perverse human characteristic that likes to make easy things difficult.

— Warren Buffett

I'm not sure how to say this, but we fly-fishermen seem to relish in the endeavor of making fly-fishing more difficult than it is. There, I said it and I can give some examples that pertain to surf fly-fishing. Oh, and I may contradict myself but I will let you know why.

We have the unique ability to overthink the smallest aspect of what we do on the wet sand and feel good about doing it. Take leaders for example. This is not fishing a 3-weight rod with a dry fly attached to a 3-weight floating line, in essence, no need for a tapered leader. A sinking line with a weighted fly will turn over just fine and the more knot connections you have the more that could fail and the more eel grass they could catch on. Contradiction, if you like to tie tapered leaders go for it.

As you gain experience, gear to that experience. I go by the gun/condom credo of, better to have it and not need it than to need it and not have it.

How you carry your gear is certainly up to you, but remember that you are now potentially standing in a hostile surf zone that is looking to eat your lunch. When the surf is big, stay out of the water and really stay out of the water if you are wearing a survival vest. You know, one of those vests that looks like a F18 fighter pilot would wear when he ejects after being shot down over enemy territory. The more gear you carry the more gear to weigh you down if a wave takes you to your knees in four feet of water. I've seen guys wearing these and I've seen guys with just a pocket with a few flies in it and one extra leader. Contradiction, wear and use what you got and then gear-up accordingly.

Fish the peak low and incoming tides. In a nutshell you can reach the structure, identify the structure and you are not standing in the washing machine, getting hammered by big surf. If you go home and your thighs are sore from keeping you upright, you've worked too hard.

Whether to go or not to go fishing? You go when you can! It'll somewhat contradict the above paragraph but here's why. Say you have only one day out of the month to go fishing and the tides don't stack up to what you are looking for, do you stay home? Nope, you go and at least see how the beaches come across. Surf too big or does this beach face a direction the swell doesn't affect? But either way you need to go look or you'll hate yourself later. Some beaches have cameras available that you can click on and see what the water looks like from the safety and comfort of your home. Think of it in these terms, you may not want to get out of that warm bed at o-dark-thirty but I can guarantee you that at 8 a.m. you'll be kicking yourself that you didn't go. I call it the "gym" syndrome. You talk yourself out of going to the gym, only to regret it later when you are sitting there bored. So go fishing…

Casting ability is the number one thing that makes surf fly-fishing what it is, fun. If you can't, it won't be but you can work on that.

Trout casting will not get it done here and you need to be able to toss a sinking line at least 60 feet to be in fish range. Fish may be closer but why limit yourself to those? Plus, what do you do when they are out farther? So what do we do? We agonize over how to get distance and watch what everyone else is doing to see if that'll help. You get your stroke down and then you see someone who gets more distance by doing something a little differently than you. Now you try to copy that, only to ruin what you already had going, making your casting stroke a mess.

I'll give you two tips on fly casting, you know that thing that can make you stop fly-fishing, come in a little closer so no one else hears… PRACTICE and don't worry about tight loops or anything else except distance without pain. If you are getting distance without pain, your loops should be good. Remember when you went out dancing and danced to a rhythm no one else heard but you had a ball each and every time? Well, go back to that mindset with your casting.

That's not to say don't take a lesson or two because those are invaluable. But we are all different: we don't drive the same cars, like the same colors or TV shows, we are all just plain different. I taught a former pro wrestler to fly cast, he was 6'6" and weighed over 300 pounds. So when he used a lot of wrist in his stroke I didn't say much other than if he used a larger rod with a heavier sinking line, he needed to use better form but his wrist will tell him that.

Then I had a 5-foot-nothing retired school administrator and I taught her to use perfect form because her size did not allow her to "muscle" any

Raphi, age 14, airing a cast out on the beach.

part of the cast. We are all different and fly casting is as easy or as hard as we make it, so relax, have fun and it'll all come together.

Once we get over the "hard" part, going to the beach is easy. Simply go to a beach and fish, it is that easy. Yes, you'll need to be able to read the water to find where the fish should be but you can still catch fish without that knowledge, just not as many and not as often. I was at a fly show once and I was talking to some people at my booth when a man stepped up and asked if he could explain how easy this is. He said he had fished the beach in the morning, caught fish and then made it to church on time. He even worked the pancake breakfast after service and he was now at the fly show at one o'clock. We all agreed that he could not have done that if he had gone trout fishing.

It is that easy so read on…

If I can do it, so can you.

Elaine enjoying retirement on the wet sand.

The fish are in the water anyways, so why not fish when it is raining?

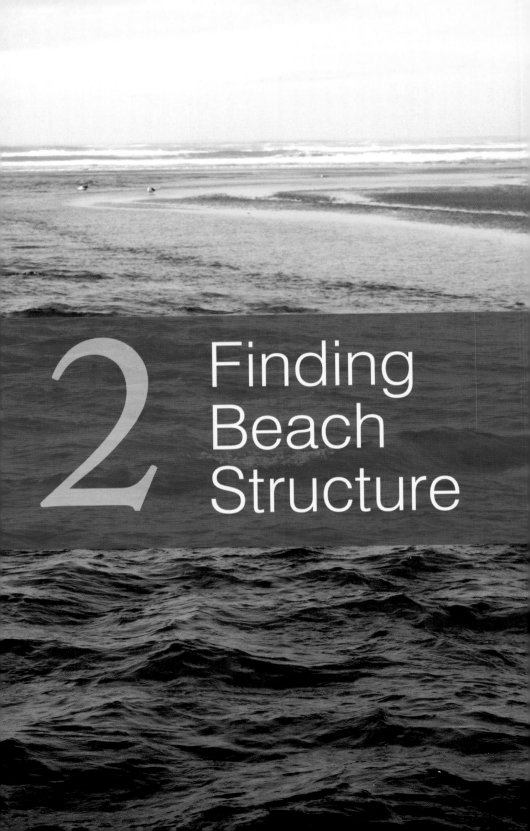

2 Finding Beach Structure

W hen Arthur Rubinstein was asked how to get to Carnegie Hall, he replied with "Practice, practice, practice."

What's that got to do with fly-fishing the beach? Well, when asked, "How you do fly-fish the surf?" I always reply, "Structure, structure, structure." Just saying you need to fish structure doesn't equate into knowing where the structure is or if it'll even be there the day you go down to the shore to fish. You can count on the seam behind that big rock on your favorite trout stream holding fish year after year, but structure on a beach is fleeting at best.

Tides, swell, wind and which direction the beach faces all play big roles in developing and maintaining beach structure. When the tide comes further up the beach, it moves more sand around than if it only came up a few inches. Add in a good-sized swell, toss in a decent off-shore gust and those waves pounding the beach can cut out holes, troughs and trenches that'll hold fish for weeks.

Find this at low tide…

...fish it three hours later when it is stinky with fish.

Although it may sound obvious, understanding that waves break in shallow water can make all the difference between catching fish or just having a nice day at the beach. The breaking or rather the non-breaking section of a particular wave tells us everything we need to know about what or who is below it. One only need to understand that all surf species are on someone else's dinner menu. This means that deep water is safe water and while these surf dwellers may feed in just an inch of water at times, they all feel safer in the deeper sections. So when you're strolling the beach with your favorite surf stick look for the deeper water, this should be—should being the operative word here—where the fish are.

Holes

Calling it a hole is a misnomer. Think more of a half moon or even a horse hoofprint in the sand only on a bigger scale. The hole will be much more pronounced towards the beach than at its back side facing the ocean where it'll taper up then flatten out, level with the rest of the sand. Identifying a hole is easy once you remember that waves break in shallow water.

Watch a wave form at any beach and you'll see a uniform line of rising water transform from swell to wave, then break as one, becoming

Good news, bad news. Bad news is this is not fishable with a fly rod.
Good news is the combination of wind, high tide and a large swell can
cut structure into the beach making it very fishable.

what is referred to as 'white water'. As you watch this uniform line roll
in, watch for a break in that line where a section doesn't roll over with
the rest of the wave but rather never fully builds. This tells us that the
area beneath this particular section of wave was deeper than the rest. As
you continue to watch, this section will only form into a wave and break
when it reaches an area where the water is shallower. So rather than
starting in Spot A, casting, stepping a foot to Spot B while stripping
your line back in then casting again and repeating this process down the
beach, we fish these holes.

Now you may ask, "How do I fish these holes?" Because 99% of the
time our current recedes to our left when facing out to sea, or downhill,
I like to get on the uphill side of the hole and cast to that upper edge.
This allows the fly to go over the lip of the flat and be stripped back

along that bottom edge. Think of the fish laying there near the bottom looking up at the lip hoping that their next meal will come tumbling over for easy pickings.

A hole before filling in. Note the darker water in the middle signifying deeper water.

If nothing happens after a half dozen casts, cast across the hole at a 45-degree angle and repeat as needed. If nothing happens after those casts, cast your fly parallel to the shoreline, about three to four feet from the shore. The incoming current will take the line and fly closer in, thus covering more ground.

Lastly, I like to stand even to the middle of the structure and cast straight out. By casting to a given hole using different angles, you effectively increase your chances of hooking up by covering more water.

Same hole after filling in. Notice how the deeper hole section has green water rather than the foam around it, once again signifying deeper water.

Trenches

Long trench with very fishable water. You can see the white water farther out beginning to roll over the sand bar, then into the bluer water of the trench. Flat section is where you can sometimes watch leopard sharks come across, green arrow shows where trench heads out to sea.

This is just what it sounds like; a long channel cut in the sand that can run for 100 yards or twenty feet along the beach. These trenches are dug out by the pounding surf and form more readily along beaches that have a steeper incline. This incline acts as a natural barrier that causes the breaking wave to dig out sand at its base, causing a deeper section to form nearest the incline. The sand that is removed from this trench is then deposited on the ocean side of the trench building up a sand bar. This makes identifying the trench much easier as waves form, break and then roll over this sand bar only to reform and break on the shoreline after building back up over the deeper water of the trench.

There are times when sand deposits can break up a trench, separate its total length, making up numerous trench sections. These separate sections also make structure on the uphill and downhill ends of a trench. Think of each end as a bay and these bays will hold fish. I find more fish on the downhill side as they have moved up against the current, only to come to the end of the line and wait for the outgoing tide so they can head downhill. Or they wait for the incoming tide to bring more water so they can swim over the sand bar and into the other side of the trench. So once again, using the knowledge that waves form and then break in shallow water we can identify a trench.

Troughs

By definition, calling this structure a trough is incorrect. While it is a low point, it more resembles that famous trademark shoe swoosh than a straight channel. Think of it as if the swoosh were reversed with the skinnier, pointy end laid along the beach and the larger, wider end pointed out to sea. Where the point of the swoosh, or apex, meets the shore is a fly-fisherman's dream.

Nearly all of the surf species that use this trough will use this apex to move up the beach as the tide comes in and fills the trough in with more water. Be it barred surf perch, leopard shark or the crafty and spookish corbina, they will all be at this point at one time or another. I look at a trough as three distinct and separate sections. One is the above mentioned apex, then you have the long channel and finally the large belly that at its widest meets the open ocean.

Standing where the apex is or where the outer ocean side edge meets the edge along the shore, forming a ">", I like to cast up onto the flat section on the ocean side of the channel. This allows the current to take your fly over that ledge and into the channel giving it a natural look. Food will be churned up and moved about by the current so it is normal for food to be swept along and deposited over these edges into the deeper water. This is where the fish should be.

If I do not find any takers here, I'll cast out into the middle of the channel and finally parallel to the shore until I find fish, all from the apex. Once again we are fishing angles of a given piece of structure to maximize our chances. The channel that extends from the beach apex to the large belly is the 'road' that the fish will use to come in from the deeper water to feed in the skinny or shallow water. At different times in the tide cycle this channel will be where the fish are and offers numerous chances at hooking up. Some channels are longer than others and some can even be thicker or wider than others depending on the depth of the water.

The beach at low tide shows the "swoosh" ready to be filled.

Green water shows structure big enough for two to fish...

…and catch. One landed and Ruben hooked up in the background.

Here I'll move downhill away from the apex, maybe as few as ten feet, and cast straight out, trying to land the fly on the backside flat. This allows the fly to be pulled from the ocean-side flat, down into the channel. If I find no willing participants, I'll fan cast, one cast to the right, one to the middle and finally one to the left, moving another ten or so feet downhill and repeating this until I find fish. I'll do this until I get to where the channel forms the belly of the swoosh and heads out. Here I will fan cast, paying more attention to the deeper middle sections.

One thing to remember here is that there is going to be some drift downhill as the current goes back out. If you cast straight out and hook a fish during the drift, you cannot simply re-cast to where the previous fish was hooked but rather you have to cast back to the original spot from which the drift started. The drift takes your fly to the fish whereas if you cast to the spot where you hooked your fish, the fly is moved out of that area before the fish can see it. So just as you may play a fade with your golf swing or adjust your cast in the wind, you need to be able to use the current to fish these areas.

Lastly you have the large belly that connects the channel portion to the open ocean. You can actually make this out by simply using what we know about how and when waves form and break. This will be the first time you can make out deeper water as the swell forms and begins to make a wave. At peak low tides, this section may be the only part holding water deep enough to hold fish. As the tide comes in and it fills in, the fish move up to the channel portion, finally ending up at or near the beach apex. This gives us three clear-cut sections to fish at different times of the tide cycle, affording us different times of the day to fish. It also gives us options as to how and when to fish.

The different sections can be fished at multiple angles to even include standing out on the ocean side of the channel at low tide and casting back towards the beach.

Swoosh before filling in.

Swoosh as it fills in.

Stand at apex and cast along seam.

Structure Doesn't Have to Be Deep

While prime structure usually means deeper water as in troughs and holes, what do you do if there aren't any of those around? You have to find structure and there is often some staring you in the face. People constantly overlook cuts and what I like to call 'rivers' running from the shore to the sea.

When the tide comes up very high on the shore, as it recedes it can cut drains or multiple channels leading to deeper water. Fish hang out at the end of these or where the surf meets the end of one of these cuts. Think of it in terms of a funnel leading right to their mouths.

If you can find a cut that has a sand crab bed on the shore side of it, even better. Now the tide will come up over this cut, the crabs come out of the sand to use the water as a way of moving to deeper areas and the currents run out of these channels. This will funnel the crabs into a mass like food shot out of a cannon. Simply stand back near the dry sand, cast your line so your line lies in the channel and your leader is in the area in front of the cut. There are excellent chances of hooking up this way and it is a much overlooked style of fishing this structure.

There are two types of "river" structure, one is a deep channel that forms a low spot between two higher sections of the sand, or what I like to call a pressure zone. A pressure zone by nature has a greater volume of water running out to the sea compared to either side of it. Fish feel this greater volume of water like they feel the tides and use it to move up to the shallower water. Some pressure zones can be very wide and deep and at low tide I like to stand near where they exit into the sea and cast downhill of it. At low tides the fish move up, or uphill, and you can find them stationed here waiting for the tide to help them move up the beach.

The other type of "river" is formed when the tide is high and it runs into a high bank. It will hit this bank, then turn downhill and run almost parallel to the beach before heading back out to sea. For fly-fishermen, this may be the only structure we find at high tide and it is very productive because the outgoing water running down the river creates a pressure zone. Once again the fish should be in this area because of the greater volume

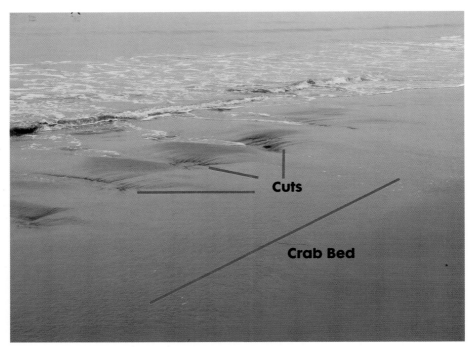

Deep cuts with a flowing river of sand crabs.

Deep cut that fish will use to access beach.

Channel moves food towards water, fish gather to feed.

of water running out churns up the sand and frees the worms, crabs and ghost shrimp from their hiding places making for an easy meal.

I could easily say that to find structure you need merely look for something different or that doesn't seem to belong there, but to the untrained eye that can be hard. It is very similar to the friend we all have that comes over to fix a computer problem for us. A few quick clicks and they say, "See how I did that?" But you can only look at them as if to say, "You lost me when you came in the door." It is very much like that, so take it slow and repeat what works for you.

No Time Like the Present

Lastly, I am constantly asked, "When is the best time to fish?" My answer never changes, it's "when you can." Be it a peak high or a peak low, different beaches fish differently depending on the direction they face and the angle of the beach slope. So the more you fish and know those beaches, the better understanding you'll have as to when it's best to fish them.

Some will fish fine at a higher tide while others fish better at lower tides. Knowing this will help you decide when and where to fish on a particular tide schedule.

If you are limited on the time you have to fish, all this data will factor in when making your decision. Most people have a job, family and the commitments that come with that territory so if you know how to indentify structure and how it fishes at a particular tide, you can totally optimize your beach time and maximize your catching opportunities.

One last thing, if you find structure holding fish, fish that structure until it either fails to offer up its inhabitants or is reclaimed by the sand. The grass is never greener and leaving fish to find fish never seems to pan out. The beach may be crawling with bikini-clad beauties or hunky lifeguards but we are there for the fish after all.

The same area at different times of the year shows how much sand can be moved by the tides.

Kelp is another issue brought in by the tides. Too much kelp in the water makes it impossible to fish because all you'll do is strip in debris.

When kelp is on the beach it doesn't cause all that many problems.
In fact it can bring in tasty little critters that the surf species like.

Same spot after winter tides have pulled sand off the beach.

Summer as sand is moved onto the beach.

A tiny spider crab hiding in the kelp. So now you know why brown flies work so well.

When kelp is in the water, it can be a nightmare. Notice how black the wave is because of all the kelp debris in it.

3 Surf Flies

Simplicity is an exact medium between too little and too much.

— Sir Joshua Reynolds

When I do tying demonstrations at fly-fishing clubs, fly shops or conventions, I always tell people that you can get as fancy as you want with your flies, or as plain. Surf fly-fishing is not about matching the hatch like trout fishing, but rather color plays a bigger part in attracting and hooking fish. Red is the number one color for surf flies, you'll see red or orange in most if not all successful surf flies. That is not to say you can't catch fish on sand crab imitations or a Clouser baitfish fly of olive over white, but color is what it's all about.

I have fished them all and for a good amount of time too. There was a spell, a year or so, where I fished an olive over white Clouser with a tinge of flash and caught all the different surf fare I wanted. Then I went to a natural colored squirrel tail Clouser and once again caught everything. But it wasn't until I started to incorporate reds and oranges into my flies that I started to really see my catch rates go sky high. The purpose of a fly is to catch fish but we sometimes need that extra little something to attract them as well. Add to that durability and an ease to cast and you'll have a fly that need not be changed if fishing slows or stops. Because that is a sign the fish have moved on.

You also need to be able to adjust to the currents in getting the fly back to you for another cast. The act of stripping the fly back is solely dictated by the speed of the current moving downhill. If that current is slow, strip slow and if it is fast, strip as fast as needed to stay in contact with the fly. You want to make sure you have as straight of a line going from your rod tip to the fly, that way you do not miss any strikes at the fly.

Checkerboards

When I picture a fly in my head simplicity in tying is always the place I start, be it a surf fly, carp fly or blue-water offering. I don't leave out functionality or durability but it's how easy it is to tie that's always first and foremost on my mind, because if it is successful I want others to be able to duplicate it effortlessly.

Checkerboard Fly Series.

Giving birth to a new fly usually begins with another fly, lure or bait in mind combined with a way of making it better through design or materials. We all want to make a fly to call our own and I did it with this pattern.

I give credit where credit is due to Brian Hastings's Surf Rat because this is a bastardized version of it. My best days landing halibut came on a Hastings's original Surf Rat of an orange cactus chenille body with a red marabou tail.

So once more I was sitting at Eric's Tackle in Ventura, California being told yet again by the conventional anglers there that to catch fish in the surf I needed a motor oil colored grub with red flakes. Being a person who loves a challenge, I vowed to tie a non-plastic/rubber copy of that grub to show them that fly-fishermen can match what they catch, but with flies. So the search began for just the right materials to replicate the motor oil colored grub, as well as a watermelon colored grub, both of which were said to be "needed" to catch fish from the wet sand.

My primary concern was mimicking the curlicue tail without resorting to actually tying in a Fly Tail, sold to impersonate the actions of marabou. Well, if they are marketed to replace marabou, why not just use marabou for my tail? So I tied on a single stalk of brown marabou the same length as the hook shank to the hook.

There's a glut of chenilles out there but I found what I was seeking in red and black variegated chenille. By adding 2 strands of red and black Accent-Grizzly Flashabou to each side of the tail all I had to do was wrap the body from the bend of the hook to right behind the black 5/32 dumbbell eyes that I placed one eye width from the hook's eye.

A pink Checkerboard fly doing its job.

I fished this fly for years, catching barred surf perch, corbina, halibut, walleye, perch, shovelnose guitarfish and leopard shark. In Baja I even landed small pargo and carbilla over the years and carp in the local canals. All my Checkerboard patterns have landed all the surf species—no one works better than the other, some just have become favorites for those who use them.

A few times I've had the name for a fly before I even tied it up and other times I fished a fly for years before it got its final moniker. This fly was named at the vise after looking at the "checked" chenille and "checked" flash that both looked like a checkerboard's black and red squares. Simple fly to tie that has excellent results. So I tied some up and I haven't stopped catching fish with them yet. The brown version has since been joined by body colors of burnt orange/yellow, fluorescent red(pink)/black, chartreuse/black, pink/silver to go along with the original red/black.

And those conventional guys who challenged me, well let's just say that when they started to use them on their spinning gear, the challenge was met.

Clousers

This is another very simple pattern that works everywhere you can fly-fish. A plain olive over white Clouser will catch all you need on the wet sand as well as other areas. Another version is a chartreuse over white or even a blue over white because both of these well work from the beach. You can change where the fly rides in the water column with an easy switch from weighted dumbbell eyes to bead-chain eyes of desired weight. More weight and the fly rides on the sand, lighter means higher in the water column so you can copy where the baitfish are at during a given outing.

One of my favorite patterns is the Flashchovie. It is a super simple pattern to tie and I've landed sharks, perch, largemouth bass, and in Baja tons of near-shore fish. Simple yet so effective and it can be used with weighted eyes or bead-chain eyes for shallower water like around rocks and reefs. I tie it on a size 2 hook and still get perch so don't be afraid to try it.

Sand Crab Flies

There are many types of sand crab flies out there and while they all work, heck, I tie four different patterns myself, I don't fish them much. I know you are asking, "but I see bait guys catch fish all the time using them." They do but a lot of times they are soaking that crab, waiting for a fish to come by and eat their stationary submission. That is boring to me. So why don't I use them? Easy, if there are tens of thousands of sand crabs blooming out of the sand and washing around, why toss another one into that mess? What I ask is this, "If you walk into a room, there's fifty women and 49 are redheads and one's a blonde, who do you notice?" Think of it as not tossing another needle on a needle stack. What I like to do is toss something out there that is 180 degrees from what is there, say a red or orange or pink fly. They easily see that amongst the millions of crabs and the fight is on.

When I do fish a sand crab pattern, I said I don't fish them much but I do occasionally give 'em a go, I like to fish them one of two ways. One, as a dropper in a two-fly rig and the other is by themselves when sight-casting to corbina.

When fishing them on a two-fly rig I like to make it as easy as possible and simply tie a Checkerboard on the leader 16-18 inches from the end. Then I tie on a hardshell or softshell crab so that it will ride up in the water column to been seen easier. The Checkerboard acts as an anchor to the lighter crab fly, giving the sand crab a lot of movement. You can tie in the Checkerboard many ways but I have found that by

My four go-to sand crab patterns.

merely tying a double surgeon's knot with the fly inside the loop works best. As you finish off the knot, keep the loop and fly together so the loop stays no more than ¼ inch long.

This will keep the two flies from tangling up on the cast but also remember to let the line straighten out more on your last false backcast before letting the cast go. In addition, I make sure to count two splashes at the end of each cast to ensure that there have been no tangles. This system has worked for me many times, especially when I put two sand crabs together, one replacing the Checkerboard fly.

I tie a Soft Shell Sand Crab, a Hard Shell Sand Crab, a Burrowing Sand Crab and the Crab Cluster. The first sand crab pattern I tied was the hard-shell pattern but almost immediately I was asked why I didn't have a soft-shell pattern, so enter the soft shell. Mine differs from others in that I use a sticky-backed felt, the same felt used on the underside of lamps and other items you don't want to scratch your furniture. It is much stronger than regular felt, giving the fly considerable durability.

The Burrowing Sand Crab came about because I don't have enough to do. Just kidding, I have plenty to do but I never stop thinking about fly patterns. I put orange painted dumbbell eyes on the back of the hook, above the bend allowing the fly to ride hook up. The felt leaves plenty of 'bite" area so you don't need to worry about getting a good hook-set. I feel fish see this as a fleeing crab because when stripped in, each strip gives the impression the crab is trying to burrow or get away safely. Fish don't like it when their food runs, so they aggressively chase it down.

The Crab Cluster is a nod to Bob Popovics' Schoolie fly where he ties two baitfish on one hook. But here I tie three sand crabs onto the hook, making sure they are stationed around the hook point area rather than down the hook shaft. This alleviates the worry of short bites or misses.

One of the earliest sand crab flies I saw was tied by my friend Dean Endress. He'd tie orange-painted dumbbell eyes on the back of the hook so it rides point up. He would shape spun tan deer hair like a sand crab shell, and then shave it flat on the bottom so it rode evenly and did not roll. This was a very effective pattern in the surf zone.

Give a sand crab pattern a try, just remember that it might be like trying to identify the penny you just dropped into the penny jar.

A yellowfin croaker that fell prey to a Crab Cluster.

Tying Instructions

Checkerboard

Hook: Gamakatsu SS15, #4
Thread: Ultra Thread 140, Red, Chartreuse, Orange, Pink
Weight: Black 5/32 Barbell Eyes
Tail: Brown, Red, Orange Marabou
Flash: Accent-Grizzly Flashabou in Red/Black, Copper/Black and
  Pearl Green/Black
Body: Red/Black, Fluorescent Red/Black, Red/Orange and Chartreuse/
  Black Variegated Chenille

Step 1: Tie on black 5/32 barbell eyes one barbell width behind hook eye.

Step 2: Tie in one marabou stalk, one and half times the length of
  hook shank, starting behind weighted eyes.

Step 3: Add two strands of Accent-Grizzly Flashabou to each side of
  marabou tail.

Step 4: Tie in and wrap the chenille from back to front, tying off behind
  hook eye to help build up nose by wrapping thread until it forms
  a cone shape. Whip finish and coat with head cement.

Soft Shell Sand Crab

Hook: Gamakatsu SS15, #4
Thread: 6/0 UNI-Thread, Gray
Weight: None
Body: Orange (Medium) Estaz, Pearl (Large) Estaz
Shell: Sticky Back Felt, Gray

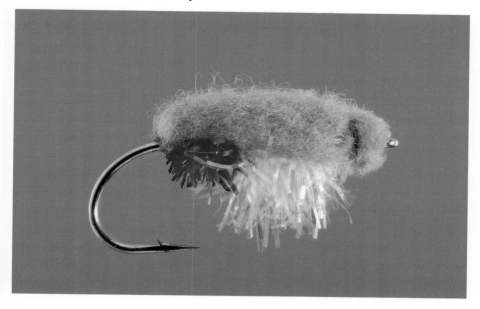

Step 1: Wrap hook with thread, tie in ¼ inch width from hook bend with orange Estaz.

Step 2: From orange Estaz, wrap pearl Estaz to just behind hook eye.

Step 3: Cut felt in a football shape an inch and a half long and a half inch wide at center.

Step 4: With sticky side up, take ¼ inch of one felt point and lay on top of the orange Estaz. Bring thread over the top from back to hook eye, wrap around hook eye twice. Stretch felt over the top to the hook eye, tie off behind eye and trim felt. Use head cement on back and front wraps.

Hard Shell Sand Crab

Hook: Gamakatsu SS15, #4
Thread: 6/0 UNI-Thread, Gray
Weight: None
Body: Orange (Medium) Estaz, Pearl (Large) Estaz
Shell: Natural or Gray Deer Hair, Solarez UV Epoxy (Hard)

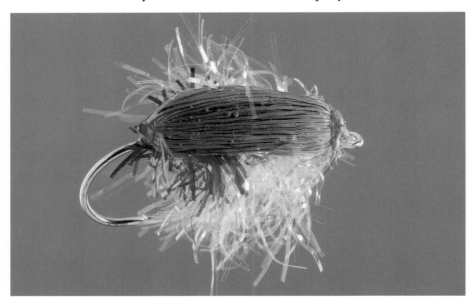

Step 1: Wrap hook with thread, tie in ¼ inch width from hook bend
with orange Estaz.

Step 2: From orange Estaz, wrap pearl Estaz to just behind hook eye.

Step 3: Select deer hair, trim ends. Take ¼ inch of the deer hair, lay
it on top of the orange Estaz and wrap around ends. Bring
thread over the top from back to hook eye. Take deer hair
and bring it from back to front, smooth out hair evenly, wrap
thread around behind hook eye, trim ends flat.

Step 4: Use Solerez UV Epoxy to coat deer hair evenly, set it with the
sun or under UV light.

Burrowing Sand Crab

Hook: Gamakatsu SS15, #4
Thread: Ultra Thread 140 Orange, 6/0 UNI-Thread, Gray
Weight: Orange 5/32 Dumbbell Eyes
Body: Orange (Medium) Estaz, Pearl (Large) Estaz
Shell: Sticky Back Felt, Gray, Solarez UV Epoxy (Hard)
Glue: Krazy Glue

Step 1: Tie in 5/32 orange dumbbell eyes at underside of hook bend with orange thread.

Step 2: Wrap rest of hook with gray thread, tie in pearl Estaz from orange eyes to hook eye.

Step 3: Cut felt in a football shape, ½ long by wide at center.

Step 4: Now put the hook point through the sticky side of the felt, spin felt so sticky side faces Estaz, tie off opposite end behind hook eye.

Step 5: Place a few drops of Krazy Glue on sticky felt end, stick and cover dumbbell eyes. Coat dumbbell eyes with epoxy so the color doesn't wear off.

Crab Cluster

Hook: Gamakatsu SC15, #4
Thread: 6/0 UNI-Thread, Gray
Weight: Black 5/32 Dumbbell Eyes
Body: Pearl (Small) Estaz
Shell: Sticky Back Felt, Gray
Line: Ten-Pound Test
Glue: Krazy Glue

Step 1: Wrap hook with thread, place 3-inch length of 10-pound test on hook, cover hook with thread, cover thread with Krazy Glue. Make a total of three.

Step 2: Tie on 5/32 black dumbbell eyes behind hook eye, wrap Estaz from hook bend to behind hook eye, tie off.

Step 3: Cut small football shape of sticky felt to fit.

Step 4: With sticky side up, put tip felt point on top of the Estaz. Bring thread over the top from back to hook eye, wrap thread around hook eye twice. Stretch felt over the top to hook eye and wrap around felt, cement thread. Cut hook off at bend.

Step 5: Tie in length of 10-pound test along one side of hook shaft so that the sand crab body rides just behind hook bend. Tie in two more, one on each side of hook bend so the three bodies form a triangle. Seal all thread with head cement.

Shelled Shrimp

Hook: Gamakatsu SS15, #4
Thread: Ultra Thread 140, White
Weight: Black 5/32 Dumbbell Eyes
Tail: Clear with Orange Fire Tip Sili Legs, Two Strands Orange
Crystal Splash
Body: Pearl (Large) Estaz
Shell: Lee's Airline Tubing Standard Size, Solarez UV Epoxy (Hard)

Step 1: Wrap hook with thread, tie in two strands of orange Crystal
Splash so they hang 3 inches off the back. Cut ½ inch off pearl
end of Sili Legs, tie in so orange tips hang off hook bend ½
inch. Tie in 5/32 dumbbell eyes at hook bend.

Step 2: Tie in 5/32 dumbbell eyes at hook bend. Wrap pearl Estaz
from dumbbell eyes to just behind hook eye. Trim center
portion of Estaz on both top and bottom of fly. This will make
sure shell fits and fly rides hook up, not able to roll because of
excess material.

Step 3: Take tubing and cut ¼ inch sections, then cut those in half,
across opening, so you get a U shape.

Step 4: Starting at rear of hook, place a small drop of UV epoxy
below hook point, set U shape with open end down on top of
epoxy, hit with UV light or sun. Place another drop at edge of
previous piece and repeat first process until you have three or
four shell sections epoxied in.

Surf Guppie

Hook: Gamakatsu SS15, #4
Thread: Ultra Thread 140, Orange, Red or Chartreuse
Weight: None
Tail: Pearl Flashabou, Red, Orange or Chartreuse
Body: Deer Hair, Red, Orange or Chartreuse
Eyes: 6 mm Doll Eyes
Dressing: Solarez UV Epoxy, Krazy Glue

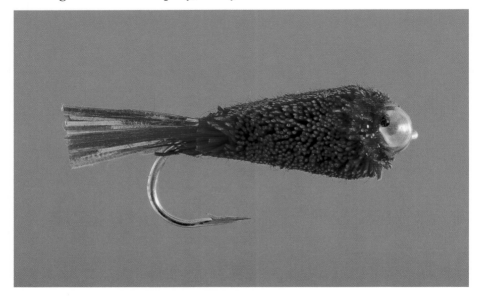

Step 1: Create a thread base 1/8 of an inch long just ahead of hook bend and tie in 15 strands of Flashabou on top of hook shank, cut to one inch long. Place a few drops of Solarez UV Epoxy (Hard) between thumb and index finger and rub into Flashabou. Move the fly into the sunlight while spreading the flash until it fans out. The tail will harden fast, hold it in the sunlight a tad longer, then you can trim it to desired shape.

Step 2: Now begin spinning in the deer hair, here I push the first bunch back over the thread wraps to hide them. Make two or three wraps of thread on the bare hook shank and then place a few drops of Krazy Glue on them to hold in place.

Step 3: Continue to spin in deer hair until you reach the hook eye, not forgetting to place the glue drops along the way.

Step 4: Begin shaping the fly's body with a double-sided razor blade. Start at the hook eye by bending the razor blade in your fingers, making an open U shape. This will make shaping much easier than using scissors. Do not cut the tail or thread. Here I make a hump on the top of the fly and cut as close to the hook shank on the underside so I have a large bite area. Continue until you have your desired shape.

Step 5: Take a single-edged razor blade or X-Acto blade, make small cuts on either side of the hook eye, back about 1/8 of a inch. Do not cut too far. Place a few drops of Krazy Glue on the flat surface and set the doll eyes in place. Coat the edges with Solarez UV Epoxy (Hard) to hold them in place, set in sun to dry.

Flashchovie Clouser

Hook: Gamakatsu SS15, #4
Thread: Ultra Thread 140, White
Weight: Dumbbell Eyes, Bead-Chain Eyes to Desired Weight
Body: Polar Flash Pearl, H2O Slinky Blend Wild Olive

Step 1: Tie in eyes ¼ inch behind hook eye. Wrap hook shank with thread back to even with hook point.

Step 2: Tie in desired amount, it varies but I like 1/8-inch-thick bunch of Polar Flash behind hook eye. Stretch back over eyes and along hook shank, make 4 large wraps back to where thread wraps end and wrap around Polar Flash 6 times. Make 4 large wraps forward to behind hook eyes.

Step 3: Take same amount of Wild Olive and tie in behind hook eye. I also make one or two wraps around eyes to hold down the Wild Olive.

Step 4: Using head cement, seal thread behind hook eye, along hook shaft and over eyes.

EBW

Hook: Gamakatsu SP11-3L3H, 2/0
Thread: Ultra Thread 140, Red
Weight: ¼ Dumbbell Eyes
Body: Red Estaz, Olive Chenille
Dressing: Red Loon UV Knot Sense

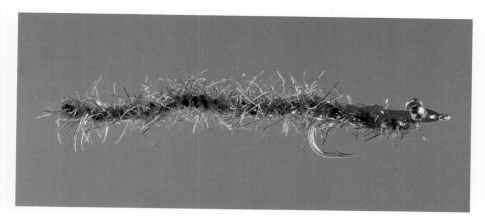

Step 1: Take equal lengths (2 feet) of red cactus chenille and olive chenille. Tie a knot in one end and place knot on fly vise. I like to use an old pair of tying scissors and place a drop of Krazy Glue on the flat section of each finger hole. Place material on glue, close scissors.

Step 2: Take scissor tip point in hand and spin to get desired twist in material.

Step 3: Once desired twists are achieved, place a drop of Krazy Glue every inch to secure twists.

Step 4: Wrap hook with red thread from hook eye to hook bend. Tie in dumbbell eyes ¼ inch behind hook eye.

Step 5: Thread hook point through twisted material so that non-glued material is over hook eye and tie off material. Make a few wraps of thread around hook bend, securing material to hook. Coat underside of hook and material with Red Loon UV Knot Sense. This will make it very durable and hold material to hook.

4 Surf Species

Variety's the very spice
of life, That gives it all
its flavor.

— William Cowper

Variety is an understatement when it comes to fly-fishing from the wet sand. If you go trout fishing, you get trout, however setting a fly to the salt can return any number of species. Typically it will be a barred surf perch of varying size and let me tell you, many a day I thanked our little friends with the jailhouse stripes for taking my fly even if they were only a mere four inches long. But fight they do, and days of thirty or more to hand are not uncommon.

There are days when it seems you can do no wrong and you land a halibut or two, maybe even a corbina but then as you bring in your fly, you see a striped bass, mackerel or white sea bass on the end of your leader. Cast your fly out into the surf and what returns may both surprise and shock you...once I pulled in a hazardous waste bag full of needles from the froth after a particularly bad spell of rain. Like it says on the curb above our drains, "Everything ends up at the ocean."

Not a surf species but you never know what you'll find on the wet sand.

Barred Surf Perch on the Fly

Gratitude is the heart's memory.
— French proverb

The barred surf perch is one of the most endearing species for surf fly-fishermen. They are abundant—found everywhere along the California coast, reaching far into Baja California—and they are fearless in their attack on a fly. They don't have a season but rather can be found cruising the beaches year round, with some months bringing 16-17-inch perch weighing 2 to 3 pounds into the wash. It's not uncommon for a two-inch perch to strike a fly an inch and a half long.

If you don't know what they're chasing that day, toss just about anything red out there and there's a good chance of hauling in a perch. More than once a fly-fisherman has sung their praises after failing to hook one of the many other surf occupants. Yes, corbina may be exciting to fight, but seeing them in the wash doesn't mean landing or even hooking one. Sure, halibut may be a delicious table guest, although finding one of legal size from the shore can prove to be a task worthy of Indiana Jones. What's great about tossing a fly for perch? Well, fishing for perch means there's a stripping basket full of chances to catch other species.

Yep, fish for perch and land a corbina, halibut, yellowfin croaker, jack smelt or one of the many different species of shark that roam our shallows. Perch may not be as spectacular as some species, but for their size they fight like no other.

Where do you find them? Everywhere is a safe answer. Preferring to feed on what the waves kick up from the bottom, these little titans like to hang out in troughs, pools and holes created by the tides. You'll know you've found the right spot when you can pull multiple fish up as they school for dinner. They are not limited to only these areas as a flat sandy beach can produce just as many fish when they come in to feed on the sand crab beds.

What are the best times to find them in these zones? Many anglers go along with the 'two hours before and two hours after the high tide' theory. This is where fly-fishermen differ from our conventional-gear brethren. While the incoming tide does in fact bring the perch in and

How's that for aggressive!

the outgoing tide will hold the fish for a time, these patterns are not carved in stone. Your better opportunities may very well be the incoming tide, but don't limit yourself to this period.

Although finding structure is the same for both conventional-gear and fly-fishermen alike, I go with the low tide schedule.

If you ask conventional fishermen they'll say higher tides fish best for them but they can also fling a 2-ounce sinker a country mile while we are limited to distance in tossing flies. Thus lower tides work better for us and here are some reasons. You can identify structure better because it's void of water. You can see the corbina, leopard shark and shovelnose much better at low tides as they comb this skinny water for food. You are not standing in the washing machine, meaning where the waves break at high tide. Waves break in the shallowest water so at low tide they'll creep in, but as the tide rises the waves break in closer as the water gets deeper nearer shore. Basically where you were standing, so you need to move back towards the shore while ending up further from the structure.

Paul came all the way from England to fish for slab perch.

Large barred surf perch.

Also when you find structure at low tide that is holding water it should be holding fish as well. So now not only do you have easy access to the structure, but also a concentration of fish. As the tide comes in and the water gets equally deep all around, those schooled-up fish move and become less concentrated.

They'll take flies in the dark of morning.

The statement that perch are around yearlong may be misleading to some. Yes, they are in the surf year round, but the quantities do slow down, along with the quality. At anytime of the year you can find perch, it's just that their size may disappoint you. There are periods where all you seem to land are fish not much bigger than the fly you tossed.

This time frame generally coincides with the appearance of halibut and corbina and the influx of warmer water. It's during these times that any fish, no matter how small, is better than no fish at all. This is the best time to try a new fly, a new knot system or work those kinks out in the old double haul.

As the water starts gets colder in October, bigger perch slowly make their way back to the beach. It may start slowly but it's well worth the wait when in late October, all of November and into December, you start hauling in the big ones. These are the breeders coming into the shallows to mate. The tell-tale sign is on the underside of the bigger perch as they have a worn black area from their chin to their tail. As the male and female line up with each other, they must hold against the current. By pressing against each other, steadying themselves on the bottom, they wear a portion of their scales black. It won't appear as a deep black but rather a roughed-up dark discoloration on their underside.

Mid way through December they start separating and heading back out beyond the breakers, leaving only the smaller perch to play with. The bite doesn't pick up again until the females start coming into the shallows to drop their fry. Perch bare their young live and this brings the larger halibut back in within range of your fly. This is a great time to be fishing.

Black marks show the spawn is going on and the
bite marks show just how hardy these guys are.

What are they caught on? Perch seem to be like largemouth bass, they'll hit anything at one time or another but almost anything in red will do.

I've tied a thin strand of red chenille on a bare hook and caught perch. Once when untangling a knot in my fly line after a cast, a perch picked a red Checkerboard up off the bottom and ran off with it. Thinking this was a once-in-a-lifetime pickup, I cast my fly back out and left it, not retrieving the fly. It wasn't even a minute before I had hooked another perch. This practice was repeated three other times at different spots with the same results. Combined with a retrieve this little chenille fly has become my favorite fly, along with the Checkerboards.

The bottom line is that the barred surf perch is a fly-fisherman's dream. They are on all beaches in good numbers; they can be taken on various flies and are a perfect choice for the beginner. You should know however that they can be at your feet or seventy feet out. I tell my clients that you need to be able to cast a fly on a weighted line at least 60 feet to catch perch with any regularity.

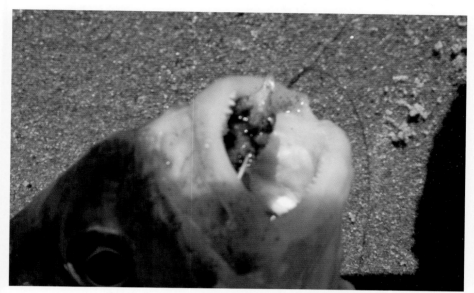

Perch have teeth that can tear a fly to shreds.

The instant gratification perch can give is a wonderful reward for the fly-fisherman who, like me, doesn't have the patience to toss a fly for hours trying for the illusive Silver Torpedo, corbina.

As of this writing, we are experiencing the best perch fishing in my lifetime. We are regularly getting 12-16-inch fish every time out on the beaches in Southern California. No one has an answer as to why the fishing is so good because we are too busy fishing. It may be cyclical and it may start on a downhill slide soon or it may last longer. No one knows because, after all, it's fishing.

Walleye Surf Perch

If you picture a crappie you'll have an idea of what a walleye surf perch looks like. They have pretty much the same shape with that same mouth that accordions out. It's that mouth that makes keeping them on a hook tough. It has a hard outer edge but between it and the head is nothing but a very thin piece of membrane. They also have slightly larger eyes and don't grow as big as a barred surf perch.

They will be in the same places you find barred perch but usually not in as great of numbers. The one thing you can count on however is that if you catch one, you should catch more. They appear to move around

Mike with a nice fish. Walleye perch have large eyes, lighter colored stripes and almost a crappie mouth to separate them from the barred surf perch.

in large schools so casting back into the same area as the one you just landed, you should catch another one. Most will be 4 to 8 inches, but I have found schools of larger walleye going as big as ten inches. These larger fish are not the norm, being in the right place at the right time is what it's all about.

Corbina

What can I say about the corbina except that it has to be the most prized surf species while also being the most scorned. Whether you call it the gray ghost, a slider or a West Coast bonefish you have to pay your respects to the corbina as the most worthy opponent you'll find on the wet sand. Many years ago we talked about corbina in terms of "follows". That is, when someone asked if you had caught any corbina lately you'd reply that you had a few "good follows" the other day. As time went on

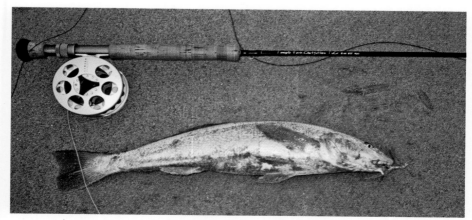

Corbina taken on a size-2 hook.

more people started fly-fishing the surf for them and that meant more people started catching them.

Corbina cruise the skinny water of the surf zone feeding on sand crabs, clams and worms. But don't be fooled by that because they are opportunistic feeders, I've seen a corbina caught on a 6" Big Hammer swim bait. I have regularly taken them on 3-inch olive over white Clousers tied on a #2 hook. So don't get taken in if someone tells you that they can only be caught on a #6 or smaller hook.

These pains in the derriere move up the coast line as the water warms up, starting well below the Mexican border and reaching as far north as Santa Barbara, their most northern habitat. As the seasons change, warm water moves up the coast and so do the corbina. In April and May those of us up north read about corbina being caught farther south, and as the reports increase and time passes we finally get our shots at them. They can be caught in harbors, on the flats of the beach, in structure and offshore near the kelp beds. There doesn't seem to be anywhere they aren't caught, with the exception of the deeper blue-water areas.

Little is known about the movements of corbina during the summer and winter seasons. Some say that in winter they head south to warmer climates, while other say they move offshore into the deeper water. Both may be right.

In January, 2005 we had a ton of rain and that rain caused a massive mudslide in the seaside town of La Conchita. It took ten lives and spread mud across Highway 1, temporarily shutting the road that runs 655 miles along the California coastline. That mud turned the near-shore water into chocolate milk and the sediment makes breathing difficult for fish. Because they bring in water to breathe, fish will move out to where they can find clear water to make breathing easier. What that meant to us surf fly-flingers was that we could not fish until the water cleared up and that didn't happen until July. So why am I mentioning this? During that time I had reports of corbina being caught offshore near kelp beds in 75-100 feet of water. So maybe they do go offshore.

Then one beautiful sunny day I was walking back to my truck after fishing along the shoreline of a beach when I ran headlong into a school of corbina. The strange thing was the smaller, 12- to 18-inch fish were being herded by much bigger corbina staying in the wave line. I moved up near the dry sand, and then I moved below them so I could cast forward past their heads. I ran head long into another group being herded just like the one I first saw. I continued to move south along the beach and saw group after group being led like this. All in all I saw over two dozen groups of smaller corbina being driven like a herd of cattle. I went back the next morning and they were all gone, but where?

When I would mention this people looked at me like I was crazy, that is until I started meeting fishermen who had witnessed this activity for themselves. So now we have good information that corbina go to deep water and they migrate. Now someone needs to get a government grant to catch and tag corbina with transmitters to prove all of this.

So what will they take as far as flies? Everything is the safe answer. They'll readily eat the same flies perch and other surf-zone species do, but they can be far more finicky than the other species. They will eat a multitude of sand crab patterns and baitfish patterns. Because they search for food mainly with the barbell that hangs from their chin, corbina have very small eyes for their size.

A smaller perch has bigger eyes than a corbina twice its size so the vibration-sensing barbell serves them well. When sand crabs dig themselves up to the surface of the sand they stick out their mouth and feelers to find food. This digging makes a vibration that corbina feel and they attack, often with their head down and their tail sticking out of the water, much like a bonefish. Actively feeding corbina will more readily go after a fly than a single fish cruising just beyond the skinny water. If there are multiple corbina feeding or cruising, your chances of hooking up increase greatly as they now are in a competitive mode for food. If you

Barbell under chin used to search out sand crabs and other sand dwellers.

have a situation like this, cast your fly far enough out and ahead of them to time the fly and corbina intersecting at the same time. The aggressive nature of the school will be to your advantage.

A couple things about corbina that I have picked up over the years. As with all surf species, I don't recommend using a trout strike, high-stick hook-set, but rather a strike to the side. Our flies are weighted and ride hook point up so if you strike with a big upward movement, you'll pull the hook from their mouths.

Tie some barbell eyes on a hook one barbell width from the hook eye and lay that hook in the palm of your hand. Grasp the hook eye and pull upward. See how it lifts off your hand with the hook point moving so it faces the sky? Now take the hook eye in hand again and pull straight across the palm of your hand. The hook point stays in place and moves in a forward motion, effectively setting in the fish's mouth.

I also tried rattles when tying corbina flies. Going on the principle that corbina go after vibrations, I laid a small rattle along the hook shank, tied it in and covered it with glue and then tied a Brown Surf Rat. I tied up three this way and caught three corbina the next day which made the experiment a success but each hook-up broke the rattle. It was cost ineffective and attempts to make the rattles more protected only made the fly heavier. So rattles do work, you just have to figure out how to make it work.

When fishing for corbina you can either blind cast—basically fish for whatever will bite the fly—or hunt them on the beach and sight-cast to them. Blind casting means you will catch other surf species but your chances of hooking corbina are still there. Sight-casting to corbina means finding them first. Here you need to be somewhat stealthy, no crashing the skinny water with big noisy steps, but rather walking with the current on or near the dry sand. You really want to stay as far away from the water as possible while still maintaining good sight on the skinny water. Corbina will face into the current just like a trout so you have to come up from behind them, cast the fly past them and at the same time in front of them and time both meeting at the same time. This may mean you cast your fly five feet past them and six feet in front of them and adjust your stripping motion to make that meeting happen.

The last and maybe most important thing is figuring out where the corbina go once you've spotted them in the skinny water. One of the reasons they are called "sliders" is the way they slide up into the skinny water only to slide right back out as the current recedes. So you get a glimpse of one as it slides back out, but where did it go? Did it slide straight out and will it come straight back in?

Remember to look for beach-goers before you make a back cast. There were plenty of people around and we were asked to leave the beach by a lifeguard. I landed this beauty on the last cast before leaving the area.

Or did it slide downhill, to your left if looking out to sea? Let's toss in a third choice and see if it slid uphill, or to your right if looking straight out. In gin-clear water you can watch the corbina's movements the whole time. Other times you have to deal with white water, caused by the breaking waves, that sits on the surface making continuous eye contact impossible. It is this dilemma that keeps us coming back for more and more frustration because when it clicks and you're hooked up and you land that fish, wow, is it fun.

This corbina survived a major bite and is healthy and feeding.

The most important trait you need if you have set your sights on corbina is patience. They can bring a grown man to his knees in surrender the way they will follow a fly and at the last split second, turn away.

There are people out there that can't wait for corbina season to start so they can go to a beach and look for them, for these anglers the hunt is the main attraction. Me? I make half a dozen casts to a corbina and if it doesn't show interest, I move on. If it really makes me mad, I'll line it. That is I cast over its back so it gets spooked. This way he is no longer there taunting me and in some small way I feel like I've won. I've caught them in every month of the year. One year I caught 29 corbina on fifteen different flies so that'll show you they are not that picky, but they do have to be feeding. I'd like to say all you have to do is get the fly in front of a corbina without spooking it and it'll hit the fly. But therein lies the dilemma.

Yellowfin Croaker

Although the yellowfin croaker is in the same family as the corbina, they differ greatly when it comes to where you'll find them in the surf and how they look. They do have a barbell under their chin but they are always silver with yellow pectoral fins and a yellow-tipped tail fin. I have never seen a yellowfin in the skinny water but that doesn't mean anyone else hasn't so I won't say it can never happen. Normally you'll find them schooled-up and running the shoreline in the deeper water.

Alan with a huge yellowfin croaker.

If the beach happens to have a deep trough inside the surf line, they will run this trough while feeding. I have seen large schools of 50-100 yellowfin croaker running the edge where the rocky shore meets the offshore sandy bottom.

You could see how fast they moved through an area, making people think the bite had stopped when actually they had moved up or down the coastline. Thing is, they'll come back. In fact, I fished one area where we found them morning after morning in the same area only to have them move off after 30 minutes. You could land 4 or 5 of them before the school would move off, so one of us went uphill and the other downhill seeing which way they went. Once one of us found them, the other would come running and we'd have that same 30-minute period to catch fish.

You'll catch most of your yellowfin blind-casting for perch but you'll know the difference when the fight starts. Yellowfin fight more like a trout, they make straighter runs whereas perch have more herky-jerky movements.

They'll take the same flies as everything else along the beach so there's no need to change flies if you want to target yellowfin.

The spotfin croaker is also in this family; they are bigger than yellowfin but their range is limited. Up in the Ventura and Santa Barbara areas, we get far less spotfin than down south below Los Angeles. Once again, they take the same flies and can be found in the same surf zone as surf perch.

A member of the croaker family. Like the corbina, both have a chin barbell.

Leopard Shark

The woman looked at me with crazed eyes as I beached my catch. Carefully removing the fly from its jaws, I took out my camera and captured a memory for my records. Setting the camera back in its case, I gently picked up the 5 feet of spots and sent the leopard shark back to the frothy wash. I counted down the seconds as I knew the questions that were going to come my way as I had been here before.

"Was that a shark?"

"Yes," I would answer.

"Do they bite?"

"No," I would reply.

"Are you sure it's safe for my kids to go in the water when they are around?"

"Yes, I get bumped by them all the time when I fish here."

"Are you nuts or something?" She would ask.

"Maybe, but they are a great fight on a fly rod, readily take a fly and are harmless to humans."

The faces of her children peer out from behind their mother's legs, mouths agape as the leopard shark swims safely away.

"Mom, I want to do that!"

That's about the time the kids are ushered off the beach and as far away from salt water as possible.

Leopard sharks are found all along the West Coast, from Oregon to the Mexican border. In April, some areas as early as March, they come inshore and roam the shore line, sometimes in large groups or as singles as the females birth their young alive. They will then spend the better part of summer feeding in the shallows where they can stay longer, well into September if the water stays warm. It is during these months, May through September, that we get our best shots at them with a fly rod. They are not alone in their lazy meanderings along the beach. Mixed amongst them are gray smoothhound sharks, picture a leopard shark without the camouflage, or as I call them, naked leopards. Either species is a kick on the fly but it's the leopard shark that gets the size. Leopard pups, up to 12 inches, will take smaller flies while the adults, up to 6 feet, like the bigger fare.

Seeing leopard sharks is much like seeing corbina in the surf, it takes time but once you've seen one you'll think you see them everywhere.

After you see the initial triangular dorsal fin poking out of the foam in just inches of water you will forever think of that when a piece of kelp flips, rolls or pierces the surface of the water. I call that being "cursed". Just try and go to the beach after seeing your first leopard shark in the shallows and you'll forever be looking for Jaws' little cousins.

I use three methods to find leopard sharks in the surf. I look for "roads", pools and finally I'll use the waves as a magnifying glass.

All Roads Lead to Leopards

I like searching for leopards at a peak low tide. This allows me to look for what I call "roads", that is any indentation in the sand leading to deeper water from the beach. This indentation, no matter how shallow, will eventually carry a greater volume of water than a flat section of the beach when the tide recedes. Fish feel these pressure zones, a greater amount of water returning out to sea, much like they feel the tidal swings, to schedule their feedings. Leopard sharks use these roads to move up into the shallow water, sometimes cruising for food in less than a foot of water. They will then return to deeper water on an outgoing road.

If you can find the road they are using to move up onto the beach, and then find the outgoing road, you have an excellent chance at multiple hook ups.

Small pup taken on an orange Checkerboard.

A three-foot leopard shark in ten inches of water.

It is at the lower tides where one can locate these areas. If you don't see any action happening at that moment, make a mark in the dry sand for when the tide moves back onto the beach. Leopard sharks will move up and down a particular stretch of beach while not deviating a great deal from their path. This makes spotting them and sight-casting much easier than one would think. Simply cast your offering into the area of these roads and wait for the tug. I often have to make numerous casts into a given zone before securing my first hook-up, but patience will pay off.

Everyone in the Pool!

Structure is the name of the game when fly-fishing the beach because, much like there are usually trout in the seam behind that boulder, there are usually fish in the holes on the beach. Deep water means safe water as all the surf species are fare on the menu of someone above them on the food chain.

So no matter how shallow the water you might see fish in, they always run for deep water for safety, meaning deeper water is where you'll find action. However just because they should be there doesn't mean you'll always find fish in these situations. After all, they call it fishing and not catching.

Once again, at low tide you get a better picture of what the structure and pools look like. If they are holding enough water, they will be holding fish. Leopard sharks like to cruise these pools for easy pickings in the food department. These pools can hold small barred surf perch, baitfish such as sardines or anchovies and small crustaceans—all on a leopard

Standing in the road this leopard shark is using to access skinny water.

shark's menu. If the barred surf perch are birthing, they birth live also, the leopards and halibut will be answering the dinner gong as both species will take advantage of the helpless young.

When describing pools this can also mean troughs of any length and shape, as well as any deep-water channel leading out to sea.

Through the Looking Glass

Not only are waves great for creating structure on the beach as they deliver and remove sand on each movement but they can also be used to spot leopard sharks. When I haven't found any structure holding leopard sharks, I'll look into the wave as it forms, staring at its base as it magnifies whatever is behind it. This is a great way to find them as they cruise the deeper water waiting to move up into the flats.

Sometimes when the tide has receded too far and there are no roads available to come near shore, leopard sharks stack up outside the waves roaming up and down the beach waiting for their opportunity to feed inshore.

When a wave builds and the water is clear of kelp, eel grass and foam, you can literally look into the wave's base and see whether there is anything behind it, like a leopard shark. Like all things this takes time and practice so that if there is a healthy amount of kelp in the water you do not spend valuable time casting to a stringer of kelp rather than a leopard shark. This is another reason why low tides are preferable to fish as they afford you the convenience of not being hammered by bigger waves as would happen at a higher tide setting.

As waves are nothing more than swells in the open water, they build as they enter shallower water and break at the shallowest point. So if you are at the beach at a low tide, the waves will form and break farther out

You might look down and see one of these beauties swimming by.

from the beach and dry sand. In essence, you can get closer to where the waves form at a lower tide than you could at a higher one.

Putting a Leopard Shark on the Beach

Over the years I have tried numerous methods to make landing a leopard shark easier and I've found that moving with the current is the best way to beach a leopard shark in less than ten minutes.

If the water is receding to your left as you look off shore, move well below to the left of where the shark has run. Keep your rod tip low, the reel pointed at the shark and while reeling, pull in towards you. The leopard shark will take the path of least resistance and swim towards you with the current. If you stand in the same spot you hooked the fish, you'll be there for an hour or more with a large specimen.

The smaller pups will come in much like a large barred surf perch in that they will make a few runs but they come in without the help of the tide. As they near the shallow water they will rebuke your efforts and head back to the breakers. You need to hold them in place as you wait for another incoming wave to help with beaching this quarry. Once you have them on the wet sand you can tail it and pull it out of reach of the water. Quickly snap your remembrance, remove the hook and pull it back to the water. The tide will do the rest and the fish will be no worse for wear. If you choose to pick the fish up by the tail, it may just turn inward and nip your calf or thigh. They have teeth and are not shy about a love bite when in this position. Tailing them onto the wet sand is much safer for both fish and angler.

If I see a lot of pups in the water I'll use a 6-weight with an 8-pound leader with maybe a bite tippet of 10 pounds to finish it off. Leopard sharks roll when hooked as a way of freeing themselves and they have a very rough skin that will cut a leader, so a bite tippet can be especially effective in keeping the connection between fly and leader.

For bigger leopards, I prefer to use an 8-weight with a 12-pound leader and a bite tippet of 20-pound, even a wire one because leopards do have teeth and a fly taken anywhere but the lip can be bitten clean off. They don't make blistering runs; rather they turn towards the deep blue and pull like a tug boat. It is during these forays that I can adjust my drag accordingly and fight them with good low side pressure as there are no coral heads or rocks, so no worrying about keeping their heads up with a high angle. Make sure all of your knots are strong as leopard sharks will test both you and your gear.

Over time I have tried flies too numerous to count and have pared it down to a few preferred favorites. An old standby, one that I have landed many sharks on, is an olive over white Clouser tied sparsely. This mimics many of the baitfish that frequent the surf and are on the leopard shark's food short list. You can tie them with weighted or bead-chain eyes depending on the water's depth. I make sure to have both in my leopard shark fly box.

Another favorite is an EBW, Eric's Blood Worm, named after Eric Huff of Eric's Tackle in Ventura, California who suggested I tie a bloodworm pattern: Take olive green chenille and red Cactus Chenille and twist them together. Then run the hook point through the twists and thread it onto the hook shank, tying it off in front of the hook eye. This fly is weighted heavily with barbell eyes so it rides deep in the sand as a blood worm would. This fly is tied on a 1/0 hook with the eyes tied down so the hook point rides up. I make a few thread wraps around the hook shank but really seal the wraps by running a bead of red UV Knot Sense along the underside, making it a very durable fly. This is my favorite pattern for leopard sharks.

Sand crab flies have worked for the pups, as has my orange Checkerboard fly which resembles a newborn barred surf perch. Leopard sharks can be very finicky when feeding so don't be afraid to switch flies often. They can also be more interested in breeding and be completely off the bite. If you see two or three smaller leopards following a larger one, they are the males chasing a female vying for her favor.

One thing that happens a lot with surf fly-fishing is that we tend to snag a lot of species. This is a result of our fly being on the bottom, our line being on the bottom and most of the surf species being on the bottom. This does not mean that these same species will not take a fly in the mouth. The better you get at spotting leopard sharks, the better you are at placing the fly near enough to them, the better chances you have of mouth-hooking this beautiful surf species. It will take time to get to where you can find these wonderful creatures on a regular basis, but the time spent will be well worth it.

An EBW at the business end of a leopard shark.

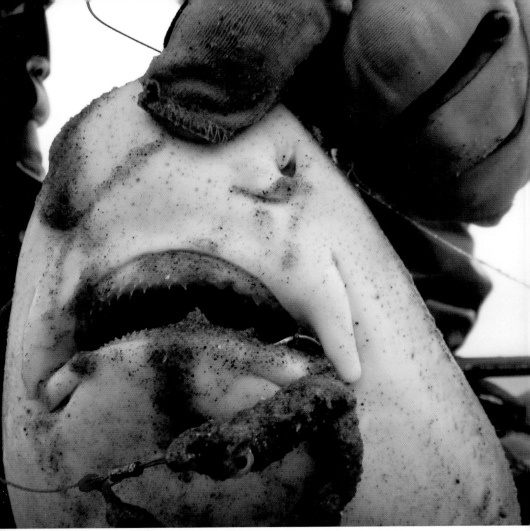

Not big teeth but lots of them give you a skinned-knee type cut, stay clear of those chompers.

Halibut

Halibut are the most sought-after food source in the surf. Sure there are a lot of people who fish for perch to eat but that's because they are easy to fool and are plentiful. But it's halibut that people really want to catch to eat. So how do they do it and what do they look for?

Halibut are caught in the same areas as all the other surf species, but there are some areas that are better than others. You can find halibut in the back bays with calm water where they settle into the sand waiting for a baitfish or other delights to swim by. Most harbors have areas of calm water behind either a breakwater or a beach well into the harbor that is a favorite swimming area for kids. Of course you need to fish there when the area is nearly void of swimmers and beachgoers so as not to hook anyone.

They also like to lie in wait amongst the submerged rocks that line the shoreline and ambush their prey. Here you have to be careful because fishing with a weighted line and fly can cause you to snag a lot of rocks and lose many flies. This is why I developed my Surf Guppie fly, made of spun deer hair shaped like a fish that, when combined with a sinking line, stays above the rocks. When stripped, it dives and then rises as you pause to strip again, giving it a ton of action.

After a rain look for drain pipes along the shoreline that have cut deep structure below them. Halibut can come into this deep shoreline water in great numbers. I found one such site and got eight halibut out of the hole one day and six the next. So if you find a hole such as this, fish it!

When hooked, halibut can feel like snagged kelp and not go into flight mode until they catch a glimpse of you. Then they run, and may do this routine three or four times until you beach them using the waves and tide movement.

Halibut taken on an orange Surf Guppie.

One last thing, I like to cast at a 45-degree angle to the beach so I cover more of the water they hide out in. Casting straight out only affords you a short time in their feeding zone.

Shovelnose Guitarfish

These fish can literally cover the wet sand as the tide recedes, scurrying back to deeper, safer water like cockroaches scatter when the lights come on. When I was a kid we called them sand sharks but most now just refer to them simply as guitarfish. You can identify them by their long tail and spade-shaped nose. This nose will be bright red from using it to dig into the sand to find sand crabs, worms and clams when they are actively feeding. Guitarfish eyes ride high on top of their flat head, their nostrils are just in front of the eyes and their mouths on the underside.

The wings at the rear of the spade-shaped head are used for altitude and descent, much like the flaps on an airplane. When hooked, they use these flaps to hold themselves on the bottom, making stripping them in very difficult. What I have discovered over time is that when they hunker down like that, I simply give a series of continuous tugs with my fly rod until I have dislodged them from the bottom. Then I use the incoming current to bring them to me. They will fight this, using the outgoing current to try and gain back the ground you have gained on them. Hold them in place when the tide is outgoing, letting them take drag if needed, then when the tide comes back in use that to reel/strip them in as the current helps you do so.

If the shovelnose is larger you'll know as soon as it takes off after being hooked, move ten to fifteen yards below it, to your left if looking out to sea, and use that downhill current to help bring the fish in. If you

Every ripple in front of the white water is a shovelnose coming in to feed.

Shovelnose guitarfish slides back out to deeper water.

stand in place on a larger fish you will not only be fighting the fish but the current as well. By moving downhill of the fish, you now use the current as the fish will swim in the direction of least resistance. Where standing in place and fighting a fish may take thirty minutes, using the current to your advantage can make the fight last only ten minutes. Also use the continuous tugging technique, a friend dubbed it the 'Baermann Bounce', to keep even the largest shovelnose from gluing itself to the bottom.

Because these fish hug the bottom as they swim and feed, we have a tendency to snag a lot more of them than we mouth-hook. You'll find the ratio to be about 5 snagged to every mouth-hooked shovelnose. Depending on where they are snagged—tail, wings or nose—they will fight differently. There are two holes near the eyes for sucking in water to push over their gills. The two holes near their mouth are exhaust ports, where the water comes out. If the route were reversed, they'd suck up sand and mud and drown. Either way you hook them this is the time to practice bringing them in the easier way by using the downward flow of the tide. They are considered a nuisance by some, but anything that tugs on the end of a leader is a good thing so enjoy those tugs.

Other Surf Species and Exotics

This is the miscellaneous surf species section, along with what I like to call "exotics". Exotics being those rare catches not normally seen or caught from the wet sand.

Rays

This encompasses thornbacks, bat rays and basically any of the other flat species. These species typically have their mouth on the underside of their body and slink along the bottom near the shore line. It is these species that warrant the usage of some sort of foot covering so you don't get strung, spiked or scared to heck when you step on one. Rays are also the reason we shuffle our feet along the bottom, in an attempt to let them know we are coming.

Bat ray with tail tucked.

Ray Fun Facts

Bat rays have a spine in their tail that will sting you and hurt. Even though they have a bumper-like forehead, don't be fooled into holding them there. Beach them with the current and then lightly put your booted foot on their tail and remove the hook, letting them scuttle back to the deep with the current.

Thornback Skates, Thornback Guitarfish and Thornback Ray

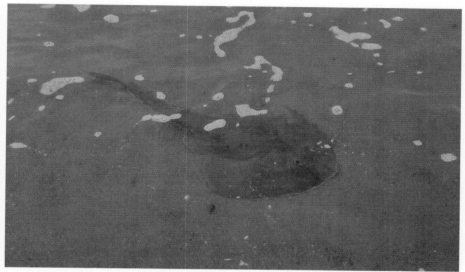

Thornback skate searching for food.

Exotics

Striped Bass

Striped bass are caught in the Southern California surf but not with enough regularity that they are targeted with great frequency. They take surf patterns but I have done best with #1 to 1/0 olive over white Clousers; my largest striper was 8 pounds.

Look for stripers where a creek, stream, river or discharge pipe empties into the ocean but they are not limited to these areas. Stripers have been caught along stretches of open beach while blind casting.

Zebra Perch

Eyes wide after landing my first surf-caught striped bass.

These fish are just what their name implies, a surfperch-shaped fish with large black stripes like a zebra. They are very rare as wet-sand catches; I caught mine while fishing a jig pattern for leopard shark.

Lizard Fish

Don't try and lip a lizard fish because they have a very good dental plan—and sharp teeth. They are also rare but I have noticed more are being landed on the wet sand as more people fish the beaches. I got mine in a bay behind a breakwater bordered by a jetty. It took an orange Checkerboard while I was blind-casting for perch.

Ugly lizard fish are showing up more and more on the wet sand.

Jack Smelt

Another incidental catch when on the wet sand. They fight well but their small mouths make taking a bigger fly tough. When you find a school of them, it's all you can handle.

I was fishing for leopard sharks when I was surprised by a zebra perch.

White Sea Bass

White sea bass have been caught from beaches up and down the Southern California coast but not with enough frequency to make them normal fare. While I have heard of a few caught along beaches, most have been caught near rocks near a bay area or in harbors. One day some years ago a few of us witnessed three extremely large white sea bass landlocked behind a sand bar unable to get out to deep water. These fish were easily four feet long and seemed very worried about their predicament, so much so they would literally swim around our presented flies. None of us hooked-up and when the tide started to come back in, they hightailed it to deeper water.

Steelhead

One of the most prized catches from the shore but illegal to harvest, steelhead are a very sweet incidental catch and worth a quick picture. I've hooked two while blind-casting for perch but failed to land either. If they are around, they can be found on open beaches and in harbors.

Bottom line, you never know what you'll catch in the surf.

5 Surf Fly-Fishing Gear

A determined soul will do more with a rusty monkey wrench than a loafer will accomplish with all the tools in a machine shop.

— Robert Hughes

Gear is a personal thing, much like the car you drive or the people you date or married. None of us use the same gear in the surf as we all have our favorites for one reason or another. So everything here is strictly my opinion on what has worked for me over the years. It pretty much boils down to what you like, what you can afford or already have when it comes to what gear to use.

My typical surf setup.

Fly Rods

Nowhere will you see personal choice or opinion more vocal than with fly rods. I believe there is more loyalty with fly rods than with a car manufacturer, even though you spend more time in a car. Whether it's the color of the blank, the type of guides used or what type of cork shapes the handle, this is a touchy subject.

One thing to consider though is that we all don't cast the same, we don't have the same body types or even the same thoughts on presenting a fly through the casting stroke. This is why I stress the importance of

Mike H. stripping in after a nice cast with a 9-foot 6-weight.

trying a rod out before buying it. They are fast or stiff rods, slow or less stiff (I use the technical term of "whippy" in place of less stiff) and intermediate rods, rods that are between the fast and slow ones. There are rods for all styles and body types, you just need to find the one that fits you. Another monkey wrench in the rod department is that not all manufacturers agree on what is fast and what is slow. Meaning that one company may advertise a rod as fast but after casting it you might call it slow. So cast as many different rods as you can. This can be achieved by going to casting clubs, fly-fishing shows and fly shops. Most shops have rods set up to cast based on what they carry, so you can get a good idea on what you'll need to make your casting as easy as possible for you.

Since we are talking surf fly-fishing we can take slow rods out of the equation unless that's what you like. Fast rods cast weighted lines a lot better, they are more forgiving in that they can absorb a mistake and help you power through it.

A weighted line loads a fast rod easier than a floating line so it makes casting that line easier. Some would think that if a weighted line loads a fast rod, a weighted line should load a slow rod much easier, and thus be easier to cast. But that is not the case as a slow rod will be slower to react, think of a worn-out shock absorber and how bouncy it gets as it gets older. That happens with a slow rod as well. The weighted line extends out on the back cast and before it can effectively load the rod, gravity has taken over and sucked the weighted fly and line to the ground before you can start your forward cast.

I prefer a slow rod for throwing floating lines because a floating line can load a slow rod easier than it can a fast rod. This is all personal as I have friends I fish with that prefer a slower rod for the beach. The need to match your style with a fly rod is very important so that you don't end up with rods that you never use.

All of the rod manufacturers have designed rods that can be safely used in salt water. More so, they have rods that can be used for both salt and fresh water, unless you are using a fly rod for small trout streams and creeks.

So what rod weight do you need for the wet sand? Whatta ya got? You can use just about any fly rod, but first you have to decide on a couple of things. If it's your favorite trout rod you may not want to subject it to the harsh saltwater environment. Think about what you plan on using the rod for and what surf species you are going to target.

For decades the standard answer has been an 8-weight. An 8-weight affords you the ability to chase everything from surf perch to leopard shark and not be under-gunned. It also allows you to fish for largemouth bass, fish the offshore kelp beds and chase bonefish. Matched with a 300-grain line it well let you fish year round, from small summer surf to the larger winter swell that comes in. This heavier line will let you keep your fly in the zone longer and avoid big bows caused by the downhill current in winter. But as your experience grows, you'll want to gear down to a lighter rod. It happens to everyone, so embrace it. A lighter rod lets you get more of a feel for what your fly is doing on the bottom because you are now matching it with a lighter sinking line. Match that to a lighter leader and you can feel when the fly pulls through a sand lip, touches some kelp or does what we're there for and hook a fish.

One thing that happens to everyone at one time or another is the dreaded flying fish. Picture yourself out there on the wet sand, you make a great cast, strip the line back but don't feel any bites so you start your next cast. And that's when it happens: turns out a perch has taken your fly but it's too small to send that message up the line. The perch is now flying by your head on your backcast, eyes as wide open as yours now are.

John G. fishing larger surf with an 8-weight.

Mike with a leopard pup caught on a 5-weight. He was fishing the bigger section of a trough, notice the apex behind him.

The trick is to quickly refocus and complete the cast so it ends up in the water, and not on the dry sand acting as chum for the seagulls.

So, how light to go? I don't like to go below a 6-weight but once again it's personal choice. I know people who use 4- and 5-weights and do very well. I stress matching the rod to your style and then the leader to your rod weight. There is no industry standard as to how heavy you can go on a particular rod but I was told by two fly rod company presidents that a too heavy a leader will not turn the fly over as well as a matched leader. I want to feel what the fly is doing while on the hunt, I want the fly to turn over easily so my casts are good and I want a leader that I can easily break off a fish that's too big for my gear.

I don't go over 8 pounds for leaders on my 6-weights because of that "feel" factor, but I also don't want to be fighting a large shovelnose or leopard shark on that lighter rod. I feel there is no reason to put the fish, or yourself, through a rigorous battle on a lighter rod.

Ariel's ready for perch or leopard shark by carrying two rods.

You may be thinking that if you use a heavy leader, as heavy as 16-pound on a 6-weight, you'll have no problem winching in the fish. This may be true, but what pressure does that put on your rod and the fish?

OK, I know I said there's no right or wrong way to do this wet sand fishing, but when I can take someone who has never surf fly-fished before, hand them a fast 6-weight rod with an 8-pound leader and they can land numerous 13-inch perch, why would you want to go heavier?

An 8-weight will serve you very well until you feel a lighter rod will give you more feel for what you are doing. Match that with a line and leader for the effort that is easiest for your style and have fun.

Now let's toss another monkey wrench into this topic…two-handed rods. These switch rods, and even Spey rods, have been tried in the Southern California surf but we don't see a lot of them around anymore. They are popular on the East Coast for getting over large surf and on wide streams with forests right up to the banks, but they are not necessary here. The natural technique for casting a Spey rod means that you leave 30 to 40 feet, or more, of line outside the last guide to cast with. On the

I have used a switch rod in the surf successfully but prefer a nine-footer.

beach we want to pull the fly in as close as needed and that can mean we pull the line to where the leader almost meets the rod tip. Fish can be caught that close and a few times each year I cheat by leaving a lot of line out, start my cast and see a corbina come out of the water, fly yanked from its lips. Not a good thing.

With a switch rod, I pull the line in as close to where I want it and begin my cast. This can be done using A one-handed casting stroke with one hand metering line out until the rod is loaded, then making the cast as a Spey rod, with two hands. It can be done with some practice, but the rod is longer and heavier. It can wear on you more than a 9-foot fly rod if cast as a single-handed rod. I've tried a switch rod on Southern California beaches and have found I don't need to do that. The longer rod makes landing a fish more difficult unless you just drag it up onto the wet sand, then pull out slack to protect the tip of the rod.

I mention these rods but if you are just beginning your journey on the wet sand, stay away until you have many years under your belt and are

Whether expensive or not, set your reel on your hat for photos to avoid that pepper-grinder sound when you reel in.

looking for a new challenge. Like I said, rod choice is personal but if you can cast many and find one that fits your style, you cannot go wrong.

Reels

You need to gear your reel choice to the fish you are going to target. If you're going to pursue barred surf perch, yellowfin croaker and walleye surf perch, an old trout reel or inexpensive composite fly reel will suit your needs. Most fly reel manufacturers have realized that surf fly-fishing is getting more popular and they have all stepped up to make affordable, quality fly reels to use from the wet sand.

Where these reels differ is in the drag systems and that is why they differ in price as well. As the reels go up in price they have a tendency to go down in weight but go up in arbor size. Saltwater reels are made for fighting bigger fish and in the surf that means halibut and leopard sharks. These two species can lay waste to an inferior drag system and even blow a reel apart, separating reel from spool. The larger arbor, the walls of the spool, can be higher for more line and backing, have a

I also use kelp to protect my reels from the sand.

larger diameter so the line retrieval is quicker. It takes longer to reel in the same amount of line on a small arbor because of the smaller spool diameter. This is very important when fighting larger fish because the extra backing you have on a large-arbor reel will handle the longer runs made by faster, stronger fish.

One of the things I've found with my gear is that I've bought to my experience and needs. I started out in the surf with a non-drag trout reel, moved on to a $45.00 composite reel with an equally inexpensive drag that handled the sand, small fish and being set on the rocks well, but blew up on its first encounter with a corbina.

By then I was fishing for larger surf species, traveling to Baja and fishing for largemouth bass so I needed a reel that could handle all those endeavors. Consequently I went to large-arbor reels that could be fished for both surf perch locally and dorado in Baja .

When looking for a reel, buy to your fishing needs. If you are only fishing once or twice a month, a less expensive smaller-arbor, heavier reel is fine. But if you plan on fishing five or six times a month, or intend to take a trip to an exotic location where you'll fish five to seven days in a row, pay the price for a lighter, large-arbor reel. That way you'll be able to fish the whole time you are there rather than taking a day or two off to rest your casting arm.

Fly Lines, Leaders and Knots

Lines, lines and more lines. There are many lines for whatever rod weight you have settled on, and for any conditions. Rule of thumb is you can cast a lighter line on a heavier rod but you can't cast a heavier line on a lighter rod. So that means you can cast that 190-grain sinking line on your 6- and 8-weight rods but you can't cast a 300-grain sinking line on your 6-weight. Casting a lighter weight line on a heavier weight rod means you have to carry more line in the air to create enough line weight to load the rod. Loading the rod is what it's all about. The more bend in the rod, the farther the line shoots. Think of it in terms of cranking a catapult all the way down so it goes farther versus cranking it only halfway down. Rod speed on the back and forward false casts, not releasing the line on the stroke, will increase distance on the release by putting more bend in the rod.

So what does all that mean? For beginners and intermediates, it means using sinking lines with short-sink tips. An integrated sinking line, one with the sinking section wielded into the fly line, with a sink-tip between 22 and 28 feet is easier to cast than one with say, a 30- or 35-foot sink-tip section. If you have a nine-foot leader and a 30-foot sink tip that means you'll have to carry that 39 feet plus a few feet of the running line out of the rod tip to properly load the rod. Carrying 40 to 45 feet of line in the air is difficult for all but the most experienced casters. Compare that to a shorter sink tip and you now only have to carry 30 to 35 feet with that line. Those 5 to 10 feet of sinking line can play havoc on the beach. A beach with a steep angle will cause you to touch the line to the ground, thus losing line speed and distance, not to mention the possibility of picking up debris like kelp to foul your cast.

The majority of surf species can be cast to with sinking lines, though some people prefer a clear-tipped intermediate line for tossing flies to corbina. Intermediate lines are lightly weighted so they will sink but if the surf is bigger than say a foot or two, the current will move that line all over the place. That movement makes it impossible to keep a fly in the area or zone the fish are in. A floating fly line makes it even more difficult on all but those days when the surf zone looks more like a lake than an ocean.

Here again we want to match the line to the rod. If you already have a rod, try as many lines on it as possible. I have clients come out with me all the time who have bought a line without trying it on their rod only to find they can't cast that combo. If you have just shelled out $70.00 for a line and you don't like it, that isn't good. This is where a fly-casting or fly-fishing club can come into play, many members will let you try lines if you ask nicely.

The most important thing is matching the line to your rod and to your casting style. It's the same as matching the tires on your car to the terrain you plan on driving on.

Leaders and Knots

Leaders and knots go hand in hand. My leaders are as simple as you can get, as are my knots. Whereas leaders can be universal, knots are as complex or as simple as you want. We all have our favorite knots so I'll mention a few that I use then leave you to your own devices. The knots I use can be found all over the Internet on virtual tying sites. Go online to learn how to tie them; in the beginning I had a hard time learning a few knots on one dimensional paper, it should be much easier to learn them on the Net.

I like my leaders a hair under 9 feet because when I hook smaller perch, say under 12 inches long, I can raise my rod tip to just behind my shoulders and the fish is right there at my chest. I take my left, non rod hand and turn my thumb to the ground, slide it down the leader and grasp the fly with my thumb and index finger. Then I turn my thumb to the sky and shake off the fish. Simple, easy and I'm not wiping slime off my hand from touching the fish.

As I have stated already, I do not go over 8-pound test on my 6-weight rods and I find no need to. Proper technique wins over winching in a fish every time. On my 8-weights I don't go over 12 pounds, even for leopard sharks. The low-rod fighting technique allows you to put a lot of pressure on a fish but not on a leader. Both leader sizes may cause you to break off a few but I guarantee you after that, you'll do fine. This doesn't mean you can't try different leader sizes, just remember you want to feel the fish, not pull in tankers from offshore.

I also like all of my sinking lines to end in a braided loop. I tie my leaders directly to it, whether it's for perch or sailfish in Baja, same set up. I run a straight piece of 8-pound or add a foot and a half of 10-12-pound as a shock tippet using an Albright knot to connect them. In the event I am using a 6- or 4-pound leader, I leave a foot or two of the 8-pound on and tie to that, also using an Albright, because I don't want to run a straight 4- or 6-pound leader.

Where sinking line meets braided loop meets leader.

Pretty simple, huh? If you are not fishing for an IGFA record, no need for elaborate knot systems. Again, this is all my opinion, but it's all been tried and tested by me and my clients. Many of whom had never before set foot on the wet sand.

There are three knots I use on the beach: the Palomar, to connect to the fly, a Perfection Loop to connect to my braided loop and the

Albright to connect leader to leader. I like the Palomar because it goes through the hook eye twice, giving it extra strength and this is important in the harsh surf environment. The Perfection Loop is simple and strong; it worked on sailfish and mako sharks but gave me a headache when I tried to learn it from a book. I couldn't see the last step until I saw the knot tied on the Web. Simple and easy, no muss, no fuss.

Stripping Baskets

There are a few different types of stripping baskets, and they are a necessary evil. When first using a stripping basket think of it in terms of rubbing your belly and patting your head at the same time. It takes some though to get the line into the basket while making a good cast and dealing with the waves and current surge. Before going out on the water, I recommend practicing your casting and incorporating the stripping basket. The more comfortable you get off the wet sand, the better you'll do on it.

We all strip line differently, so you'll need to find your natural hand movement. To do this position your stripping basket in front of you to match where your hand naturally pulls down. Most of us don't pull straight down so having the basket squared up in front will not be the optimal position. Most people tend to pull it to one side or the other, right-handers pull towards the left so we place our baskets a smidge to the left, near our hip. This places the basket in position to receive the line in one smooth motion.

There are four types of stripping baskets: homemade, mesh, hard plastic and foam. They each have pros and cons that will fit your particular needs.

The homemade basket is whatever you make it. You can make it large or small, deep or shallow, but you will need a belt to hold it up. You'll want to either drill holes in the bottom of your basket or get one that is slotted so water drains out of it. I've even seen a guy using a bungee cord to hold his stripping basket up. You also need some sort of fly-line coil separators. This can be simple zip ties put through the bottom so the memory coils are split apart.

Next we have the mesh baskets. There are a few on the market and they all work well unless you wear a fanny pack. The fanny pack would

You can see the zip ties added for coil control.

go on over the basket's belt pushing the top of the basket downward, creating less area to put line in. Also, mesh baskets will need separators added just like the homemade basket.

Mesh baskets pack well, some are designed to fold into themselves taking up very little room. If you use a fanny pack it well interfere with the mesh basket some, but if you wear a vest or carry your extra flies and leaders in your waders they work great.

Orvis is the only manufacturer making a hard-plastic stripping basket in the US and it comes with everything you need except holes in the bottom. It has separating cones and a good belt, rides well on the hip or squared-up in front of you. It even has lowered side sections so you can rest your rod across the basket. When putting holes in the bottom don't go too big. People think the bigger the holes, the faster the water will run out. Yeah, that will happen but if you drop a fly in the basket out the bottom it'll go if the holes are too big. I prefer more holes of a smaller diameter than fewer bigger holes.

I've heard some say that you can't pack a plastic basket, but I simply put the basket in my suitcase and pack the items in it. No problem at all to bring it along on any trip.

The Orvis basket.

The last basket type is made of hard foam. As of this writing this basket is not available while they are looking for a new manufacturer to take over production. Too bad, because I prefer this type of basket; I wear a fanny pack so it works well with that setup. This basket doesn't need a belt, it has a metal clip that you attach to a wading belt, fanny pack belt, even an old belt you have laying around. This basket comes apart for packing, the bottom comes out and the basket folds flat. The bottom has holes so the water goes out, with smaller holes built in for the separating cones that come with it. They are manufacturing this again but without the clip, it now uses a belt.

There is another plastic basket but it's from Denmark. The Linekurv is a great basket but you still need to drill drain holes in it. It has a larger basket area than the rest and by being bigger, fits well on the body whether squared-up or off center. This is what I have been using and I love it.

So which basket is for you?

The homemade one is what you make it, so if it isn't what you want, you're to blame.

Mesh baskets tend to wear out sooner than the others if used a lot and need more tweaking to be fully functional.

The Orvis/LineKurv baskets are great to use and you can place a fish in it to take a picture without any trouble. However, if used with a fanny pack the two belts tend to intertwine so quick removal can be a problem.

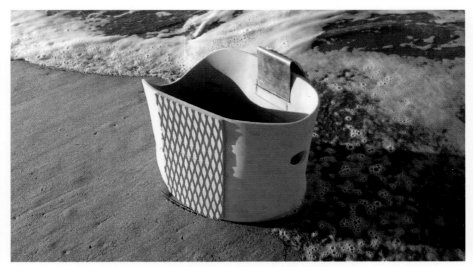

I sure hope this comes back into production.

If the hard-foam basket is manufactured again it will definitely be a good thing. While you can put a fish in it to take a photo, this basket is a bit deeper than the Orvis/LineKurv baskets so the fish doesn't lay flat.

One drawback with most of these baskets arises with the need to periodically use the little boy's rock. You have to reel in your line with every basket but the foam one if you want to take it off to do your business. This may not seem like a big deal but if you have the perfect amount of line out, getting that same amount out again can be tough. And if you are fighting a big leopard shark, dumping the basket on the sand to move freely up and down the beach is much easier with the hard-foam basket.

So if you are going to fly-fish the surf, you need to get a basket and you'll need to see which one fits your needs best. If not, you'll be doing the line dance as the free line tangles around your feet with the movement of the tide.

Plenty of room in this Dutch import.

It's the End, Go Fishing!

One of the things I constantly stress to my clients is to have fun and relax. There are too many things already going on in our lives to confuse us without making fly-fishing the surf more difficult than it has to be. I really hope you get something from this book so that it does become easier for you. Stop to enjoy what's around you. People pay big money to see what you can for free.

A Few Final Thoughts

There are three aspects to surf fly-fishing: casting the fly out, putting it where the fish should be and getting the fly back. Mess up one and it can mean no fish.

When casting, open your stance (keep the foot on your rod hand side pointed straight or you can over-rotate and cross your body on line release) and watch your back cast. That way you do not lower your arm and you can also watch the line so that you get the same amount, correct amount, of colored running line out to load the rod. Do that every time and your casting will get you fish.

Don't over-think it. Red flies and simple leaders win the day and give you more time to fish.

Remember to bounce your rod tip to quickly land those pesky shovelnose.

Strip in your fly by letting the current dictate the speed. The fish don't care how fast or slow you go.

Yes, you do need to use that stripping basket you hate. Kelp, eel grass and even dogs make it a necessary evil.

Watch out for beach-goers because they will not be watching out for you.

Finally, have fun . . . and if you aren't, email me at flyfishthesurf@ yahoo.com and I'll see what I can do to help out.